W9-CMH-363

ASTRONOMY, ASTRONAUTS, and SPACE EXPLORATION

CRABTREE
Publishing Company
www.crabtreebooks.com

Crabtree Publishing Company
www.crabtreebooks.com
1-800-387-7650

Published in Canada
Crabtree Publishing
616 Welland Avenue
St. Catharines, ON
L2M 5V6

Published in the United States
Crabtree Publishing
PMB 59051
350 Fifth Ave, 59th Floor
New York, NY 10118

Author: Clive Gifford
Editorial director: Kathy Middleton
Editors: Izzi Howell, Shirley Duke
Designer: Clare Nicholas
Cover design and concept: Lisa Peacock
Proofreaders: Kathy Middleton
Prepress technician: Ken Wright
Print and production coordinator: Margaret Amy Salter

Published by Crabtree Publishing Company in 2016

First published in 2015 by Wayland
Copyright © Wayland, 2015

Printed in the USA/082015/SN20150529

Picture credits:
Shutterstock/nienora cover (background), Shutterstock/Vadim Sadovski cover (tl), Shutterstock/notkoo cover (tl), Shutterstock/Antony McAulay cover (c), Shutterstock/godrick cover (bl), Shutterstock/Petrafler cover (bl), Shutterstock/Fer Gregory cover (br), Shutterstock/A-R-T title page (background), NASA title page (centre).

Thinkstock/hugocorzo 4 (bl), Shutterstock/oorka 4 (br), Shutterstock/Asmus 5 (tr), Shutterstock/andromina 5 (bl), Shutterstock/Tribalium 5 (br), Justus Sustermans/Wikimedia 6 (tr), Kerry Flaherty and Q2A Solutions 6 (br), English School, [c.1715-1720]/Wikimedia 7 (tr), Kerry Flaherty and Q2A Solutions 7 (cl), Shutterstock/Bryan Solomon 7 (br), Gordon Chesterman - www.gcmediatenerife.com 8 (bl), Shutterstock/Kapreski 8 (br), NASA/ Jim Ross 9, Kerry Flaherty and Q2A Solutions 10, NASA/Goddard/SDO AIA Team 11 (tr), NASA/JPL-Caltech and The Hubble Heritage Team (STScI/AURA) 11 (br), Shutterstock/Manamana 12 (l), NRAO/AUI/NSF 12 (r), National Science Foundation 13 (cl), Shutterstock/RedKoala 13 (cr), Shutterstock/Fenton one 13 (bl), NASA 14 (bl), Raghvendra Sahai and John Trauger (JPL)/the WFPC2 science team/NASA 14 (br), NASA/Ball Aerospace 15 (tr), Shutterstock/RedKoala 15 (bl), NASA 16, NASA 17 (tr), Shutterstock/Alhovik 17 (cl), Shutterstock/andromina 17 (br), NASA/JPL-Caltech/UCLA/McREL 18 (tr), Shutterstock/PrOlena 18 (bl), ESA 19 (tr), NASA/LEGO 19 (bl), Shutterstock/Mickicev Atelje 19 (br), NASA/JPL-Caltech/UMD 20, NASA/JPL-Caltech 21 (c), Shutterstock/WonderfulPixel 21 (bl), NASA 22 (tr), Shutterstock/bioraven 22 (bl) NASA 23 (c), Shutterstock/joingate 23 (br), NASA 24, Shutterstock/bioraven 25 (tr), NASA 25 (bc), NASA 26, NASA 27 (tr), Shutterstock/Swill Klitch 27 (bl), Shutterstock/andromina 27 (br), NASA 28 (bl), Shutterstock/RedKoala 28 (br), NASA 29.

Design elements throughout: Shutterstock/PinkPueblo, Shutterstock/topform, Shutterstock/Nikiteev_Konstantin, Shutterstock/Vadim Sadovski, Shutterstock/ Shutterstock/Elinalee, Shutterstock/mhatzapa, Shutterstock/notkoo, Shutterstock/Hilch.

Library and Archives Canada Cataloguing in Publication

Gifford, Clive, author
    Astronomy, astronauts, and space exploration / Clive Gifford.

(Watch this space!)
Incudes index.
Issued in print and electronic formats.
ISBN 978-0-7787-2021-8 (bound).--ISBN 978-0-7787-2025-6 (pbk.).--
ISBN 978-1-4271-1688-8 (pdf).--ISBN 978-1-4271-1684-0 (html)

    1. Astronautics--Juvenile literature. 2. Space flight--Juvenile literature. 3. Manned space flight--Juvenile literature. 4. Astronauts--Juvenile literature. 5. Astronomy--Juvenile literature. I. Title.

TL793.G54 2015   j629.4   C2015-903181-8
                                        C2015-903182-6

Library of Congress Cataloging-in-Publication Data

Gifford, Clive, author.
 Astronomy, astronauts, and space exploration / Clive Gifford.
   pages cm. -- (Watch this space!)
"First published in 2015 by Wayland."
 Includes index.
 ISBN 978-0-7787-2021-8 (reinforced library binding : alk. paper) --
ISBN 978-0-7787-2025-6 (pbk. : alk. paper) --
ISBN 978-1-4271-1688-8 (electronic pdf : alk. paper) --
ISBN 978-1-4271-1684-0 (electronic html : alk. paper)
1. Astronomy--Juvenile literature. 2. Observatories--Juvenile literature. 3. Astronauts--Juvenile literature. 4. Outer space--Exploration--Juvenile literature. I. Title.

QB46.G475 2016
520--dc23
                                        2015015366

CONTENTS

STARGAZING

Just as we do, ancient people looked up and marveled at the night sky. Some went further, studying the movement of stars and planets to navigate or build accurate calendars. Over time, the investigation of the night sky became the science of astronomy.

Tracking Movement

Changes in the patterns of stars, caused by Earth's orbit around the Sun, were charted by past civilizations to predict the seasons. The ancient Egyptians knew when the Nile River would flood farmland each year by the position of the star Sirius, which they called the Star of Isis.

ANCIENT BELIEFS

The ancient Egyptians believed that the Sun was a god called Ra, who was swallowed every evening by a night-sky goddess called Nut. The ancient Chinese were fearful of solar eclipses because they believed that a giant dragon had eaten the Sun.

WHO WERE HO AND HSI?

According to legend, Ho and Hsi were ancient royal astronomers in China, responsible for predicting when solar eclipses would occur. When they failed to predict the eclipse in 2136 BCE, the emperor had them executed!

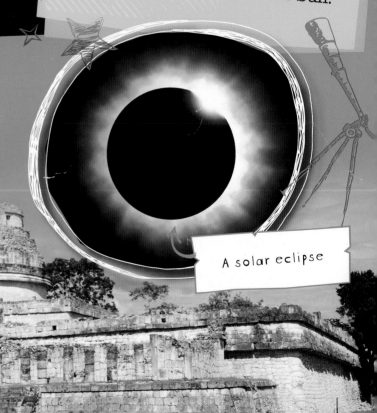

A solar eclipse

This Mayan observatory was built around 906 CE. Mayan astronomers were able to predict the length of Venus's orbit around the Sun to within two hours without telescopes.

Great Greeks

The ancient Greeks made many important discoveries. For example, Aristarchus figured out that Earth spins on its own axis, and Thales predicted a solar eclipse. The ancient Greeks also gave us the term planet, from *planētēs*, meaning wanderer. This was inspired by the planets' movement across the night sky.

AMAZING BRAHE

Tycho Brahe was a 16th-century Danish nobleman who was fascinated by astronomy. Over years of observation, he built up an incredibly accurate catalog of over 960 stars—all spotted with the naked eye since telescopes had not yet been invented. Brahe's assistant, Johannes Kepler, would go on to prove that planets **orbit** the Sun in an oval path.

This is a statue of Tycho Brahe in Copenhagen, Denmark.

36

= THE NUMBER OF STARS DETAILED IN THE OLDEST KNOWN STAR CATALOG, CALLED *THREE STARS EACH.* IT WAS WRITTEN ON CLAY TABLETS BY THE ANCIENT BABYLONIANS MORE THAN 3,200 YEARS AGO.

Tycho Brahe lost much of his nose in a duel, but made himself a false nose out of metal and wax!

OPTICAL TELESCOPES

The first telescopes were invented around 1608 by Dutch spectacle makers, who placed glass lenses in a tube to magnify objects. Many early telescopes were used by merchants and sailors to spot distant ships.

Looking Up

The Italian scientist Galileo Galilei did not invent the first telescope, but he was one of the first to point it skyward. He detected sunspots on the Sun's surface and was the first person to see Jupiter's four largest moons: Io, Callisto, Ganymede, and Europa.

Galileo Galilei
1564–1642

REFRACTING TELESCOPES

Galileo's telescope was a **refracting** telescope, gathering in light through an **aperture** of about a half inch (1.5 cm)—around twice the size of of an eye's pupil. The bigger the aperture, the greater the amount of light let in by it. When people started building telescopes with bigger apertures and lenses, they could see distant objects in greater detail.

Refracting telescope

4. The eyepiece lens magnifies the image.

1. Light travels through the aperture.

3. Light meets at the focal point.

2. The objective lens bends (refracts) light, focusing it.

Mirror, Mirror

In 1668, English physicist Sir Isaac Newton was the first person to make a **reflecting** telescope by replacing lenses with mirrors. It proved to be a practical design since it didn't need a huge aperture to see distant objects. Mirrors also weigh less than lenses, create less distortion, and are easier to make at large sizes.

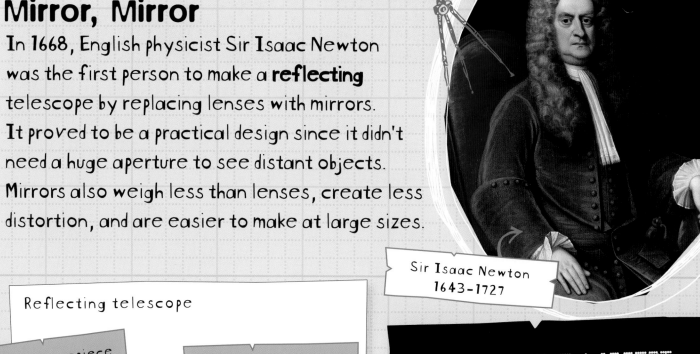

Sir Isaac Newton
1643-1727

Reflecting telescope

4. The eyepiece lens magnifies the image.

3. The secondary angled mirror directs light to the eyepiece.

1. Light enters the telescope.

2. The main mirror bends light and sends it to the secondary mirror.

HOW BIG IS THE LARGEST REFLECTING TELESCOPE?

Currently, the largest reflecting telescope is the Gran Telescopio Canarias, with a mirror diameter of 34 feet (10.4 m). However, telescopes with mirrors up to 132 feet (40m) in diameter will be possible within the next ten years.

TELESCOPES TODAY

The giant 32-foot (10 m) aperture and mirror of the Keck I telescope allow it to peer into deep space. But when linked to its twin, Keck II, the pair of telescopes can see even farther. In 1999, the Keck telescopes were the first optical telescopes to view an **exoplanet** and spot stars swirling around the giant **black hole** at the center of the Milky Way galaxy.

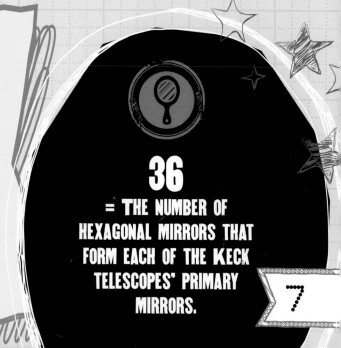

36
= THE NUMBER OF HEXAGONAL MIRRORS THAT FORM EACH OF THE KECK TELESCOPES' PRIMARY MIRRORS.

OBSERVATORIES

Large telescopes are often housed with computers and special cameras in observatories. These are built in remote locations, away from cities whose lights could interfere with observations, and in dry places with few clouds to get in the way.

Remote Controlled

Observatories build telescopes inside protective domes that open up for viewing. Computers control the precise position of the telescope. Some, like the Bradford Robotic Telescope in the Canary Islands, can be controlled from anywhere in the world by instructions sent over the Internet.

SHAPING UP

The air in the atmosphere above a telescope is constantly moving, which can blur images. Some scientific telescopes overcome this by using adaptive optics. This technology consists of a computer and additional mirror that can change shape according to the air movement, helping to sharpen the telescope's images.

The Bradford Robotic Telescope is shown scanning the Milky Way galaxy.

26

= THE NUMBER OF DIFFERENT TELESCOPES HOUSED AT THE KITT PEAK NATIONAL OBSERVATORY IN ARIZONA— THE LARGEST GROUPING OF ASTRONOMICAL INSTRUMENTS IN THE WORLD.

Splitting Light

Observatories also feature other instruments besides telescopes. They include photometers, which measure how bright an object is, and spectrographs, which divide up light coming from a star or another object into different colors called a spectrum. Astronomers can analyze spectrums to learn what gases an object is made up of.

HOW OLD IS THE OLDEST OBSERVATORY?

Many ancient people built places to observe the stars and planets. The oldest of these observatories is the Goseck Circle in Germany. Used to map the Sun's path, it is over 6,800 years old!

TAKE-OFF TELESCOPE

A modified Boeing 747 has been turned into a flying observatory that can travel above Earth's **atmosphere** to obtain a clearer view of space. Called SOFIA, the US–German observatory has a 8.2-foot (2.5 m) reflecting telescope and instruments to study the infrared waves given off by newborn and dying stars.

SOFIA is shown here flying over the Sierra Nevada Mountains in the United States.

DLR

N747NA

SOFIA's telescope door can be opened while in flight.

SEEING OTHER WAVES

Gamma rays, X-rays, and radio waves are all types of electromagnetic radiation. Although invisible to our eyes, they can be collected and studied by astronomers using special instruments.

The Electromagnetic Spectrum

Each type of electromagnetic radiation, from radio waves to gamma rays, has its own wavelength. A wavelength is the distance between a point on one wave and the same point on the next wave. The shorter the wavelength, the greater the energy produced by the radiation. These wavelengths can be plotted on an electromagnetic spectrum.

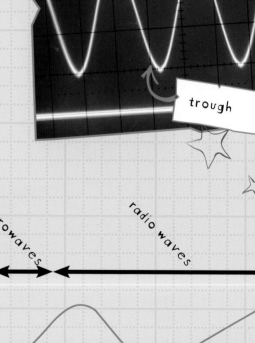

wavelength

crest

trough

visible light

gamma rays   X-rays   ultraviolet   infrared   microwaves   radio waves

wavelength

more energy   less energy

X-RAYS

Very hot stars measuring temperatures of 1,800,000°F (1,000,000 °C) or higher give off large amounts of X-rays. Exploding stars also produce X-rays. Instruments that track X-rays can record giant star explosions.

An ultraviolet image of the Sun

ULTRAVIOLET

Ultraviolet waves are shorter and have more energy than visible light. Many of the hottest stars in the universe give out most of their energy in the ultraviolet range.

GAMMA RAYS

Gamma rays have the shortest wavelength but the highest energy of all electromagnetic waves. They are released by the most energetic actions occurring in the universe, such as **matter** falling into a black hole. Most gamma rays are absorbed by Earth's atmosphere, so gamma-ray telescopes are either sent into space or carried high above Earth in high-altitude balloons.

INFRARED

Cooler objects in space, like comets, give off infrared radiation. This has less energy than visible light, but can be spotted and measured using infrared telescopes.

An infrared image of the Sombrero Galaxy

RADIO ASTRONOMY

Radio waves have the longest wavelengths of all types of electromagnetic radiation. They travel through Earth's atmosphere and can be tracked by radio telescopes on the ground.

DIY Discoveries

Between 1937 and the mid-1940s, Grote Reber was the world's only radio astronomer! He built the first radio dish out of sheet metal and parts from an old Model T Ford truck, next to his mother's house in Chicago. Using his 32-foot- (9.75 m) wide dish, Reber made the first radio survey of space, discovering radio waves coming from many galaxies.

SEEING THE INVISIBLE

Many radio waves come from the cool gas found between stars that cannot be seen by optical telescopes. Radio waves travel through dust, so radio astronomy is incredibly useful for studying dusty areas of space, such as stellar nebulae, which are clouds of dust and gases, or the centers of some galaxies.

WHAT HAVE WE DISCOVERED THROUGH RADIO ASTRONOMY?

Radio astronomy has led to many discoveries, including a type of dense, fast-spinning star called a pulsar. Radio telescopes have also detected giant jets of gas shooting out from distant galaxies. The jet shooting from the center of the M87 galaxy is thought to be 5,000 light-years long!

(Left) The Very Large Array (VLA) is a modern radio astronomy observatory made up of 27 radio antennas.

This is the very first radio dish.

Dishing It Up

Radio waves from space are usually collected using large, **concave** radio antenna dishes. Scientists increase the strength of the signals to measure them. To gather more radio waves, bigger dishes can be built, or a series of small to medium-sized dishes can all work together, grouped in what astronomers call an array.

HEY, HEY, IT'S AN ARRAY!

The Square Kilometer Array (SKA) will be the world's biggest radio telescope when completed in the 2020s. It will feature thousands of small antennas working together, located mostly in Australia and South Africa. It's combined area for collecting waves will be about 0.4 square miles, or one square kilometer.

189 (305)
= THE DIAMETER IN MILES (KM) OF THE LARGEST SINGLE RADIO TELESCOPE DISH. THE DISH, LOCATED AT THE ARECIBO OBSERVATORY IN PUERTO RICO, IS MADE UP OF OVER 38,000 ALUMINUM PANELS JOINED TOGETHER.

One of the jobs the radio telescope dish at the Arecibo Observatory is used for is to find signals from extraterrestrial life.

Huge amounts of computing power will be needed to process signals from the SKA's antennas. The array's main computer will have as much power as 100 million personal computers!

OBSERVATORIES IN SPACE

Earth's atmosphere can distort, or alter, visible light coming from space, as well as block out other electromagnetic waves, such as gamma rays. To avoid these observation problems, telescopes and scientific instruments have been launched high above the atmosphere to view space.

The Hubble Space Telescope

The most famous space observatory of all is the 52-foot- (15.9 m) long, 12.1 ton (11 metric ton) Hubble Space Telescope. Launched in 1990, it orbits 347 miles (559 km) above Earth's surface. The instruments onboard the Hubble can view ultraviolet, infrared, and visible light, and are specially designed to require very little electricity. The Hubble operates on only 2,800 watts of power—about the same amount as starting a microwave oven.

SNAP-HAPPY

The Hubble's powerful cameras have taken some of the most spectacular images ever seen of distant objects in space. Each week, the Hubble transmits around 120 gigabytes of images and data back to its command center on Earth. By 2014, it had taken over 750,000 images of stars, galaxies, and other bodies.

The Hubble Telescope captured this stunning hourglass pattern around a dying star.

The Hubble Telescope orbits Earth.

Hot and Cold

Launched into space in 1999, the Chandra Observatory gathers X-rays given off by incredibly hot objects in space, like the remains of exploding stars. In contrast, the Spitzer space telescope investigates cooler objects in space that give off infrared energy. Since its launch in 2003, Spitzer has spotted and tracked new comets, and discovered the largest, faintest ring around Saturn.

Scientists are shown here assembling parts of the Spitzer telescope.

342 (550)
= THE DISTANCE IN MILES (KM) FROM WHICH THE JWST WOULD BE ABLE TO SPOT A FOOTBALL-SIZED OBJECT. IT IS APPROXIMATELY SEVEN TIMES MORE POWERFUL THAN THE HUBBLE.

FOLD-OUT OBSERVATORY

The James Webb Space Telescope (JWST) is the Hubble's successor, with its launch planned for 2018. Both the observatory's 21.3-foot (6.5 m) mirror and its 59x40-foot (18x12.2 m) protective sun shield (a little smaller than a tennis court!) are far too big to fit inside a rocket. They have been designed to fold up for launch, and then automatically fold out once the observatory is in space.

LIFT-OFF!

Getting machines past Earth's gravity and into space takes a HUGE amount of power. There's only one type of engine capable of generating enough thrust, or pushing force, to counteract the force of gravity and launch a spacecraft into space. That is a rocket engine.

Action-Reaction

Rocket engines work on the principle that for every action there is an equal and opposite reaction. When a rocket engine burns fuel, it generates gases that blast downward out of the engine's exhaust (the action), forcing the rocket to travel in the opposite direction (the reaction)—upward!

SOLID OR LIQUID

There's no oxygen-rich air in space to keep fuel burning, so rockets have to carry their own oxygen or oxygen-creating chemicals, known as oxidizers, with them. These are mixed with the fuel and then burned. The Saturn V rocket burns over 33,069 pounds (15,000 kg) of fuel and oxidizer each second when lifting off—more than the weight of two adult elephants.

The Apollo 11 Saturn V rocket heads into space.

Getting A Boost

Some launch vehicles gain extra power from external, or outside, rocket engines called boosters. These fire at launch and fall away minutes later after using up all their fuel. The two boosters used to launch the Space Shuttles generated enough energy in their first two minutes of firing to heat 87,000 homes for a day.

The Space Shuttle Challenger launches for the first time in 1981.

PAYLOADS

Rocket engines power launch vehicles that contain objects to be carried into space. These objects are called the **payload**. This may be a **space probe** or a manned spacecraft. The first living payload in space was a small collection of fruit flies sent into space in a V2 rocket in 1947.

WHAT IS THE BIGGEST-EVER LAUNCH VEHICLE?

NASA's Saturn V rocket was 34.7 feet (10.6 m) wide and 360.8 feet tall (110 m)—taller than the Statue of Liberty. Its engines produced approximately 7.5 million pounds (3.4 million kg) of thrust at lift-off.

133

= THE NUMBER OF SUCCESSFUL MISSIONS MADE BY NASA'S SPACE SHUTTLE REUSABLE LAUNCH VEHICLES. SPACE SHUTTLES BLASTED UP INTO SPACE USING ROCKET ENGINES, AND GLIDED BACK DOWN TO EARTH CARRYING UP TO SEVEN CREW MEMBERS.

SPACE PROBES

Space probes are machines sent on a one-way mission to explore space. Most probes never return to Earth. Probes don't need a lot of equipment, supplies, or life-support systems, since they don't carry people. They can be built smaller and cheaper than human-carrying spacecraft because they only need a power source.

Super Solar

Space probes are powered by solar panels or by generators that use radioactive elements as fuel. Probes send back data, digital images, and measurements to Earth through radio waves.

This illustration depicts the DAWN probe orbiting the asteroid Vesta.

FLY-BY

Many probes are designed to fly past planets, moons, asteroids, or comets, taking measurements as they travel. NASA's Voyager 2 performed fly-bys of Jupiter, Saturn, Uranus, and Neptune. The DAWN probe performed a fly-by of Mars before orbiting the large asteroid Vesta and visiting the dwarf planet Ceres.

In 2011, the Lunar Reconnaissance Orbiter (LRO) space probe sent back 192 terabytes of photos and other information as it orbited the Moon—enough to fill 41,000 DVDs.

WHAT'S THE FARTHEST A SPACE PROBE HAS EXPLORED?

The Voyager 1 space probe was launched in 1977 and is still traveling. It is now over 12 billion miles (19 billion km) from Earth.

Locked In Orbit

Some space probes are sent to a planet or moon and go into orbit around it so they can study and photograph it. The Mars Express probe has been traveling around Mars since 2003, sending back huge amounts of information about the planet's atmosphere and surface. It has even performed a fly-by of Phobos, one of Mars's two moons.

This illustration depicts the Philae probe on the surface of Comet 67P/C-G.

LONG-TERM RELATIONSHIP

In 2014, after a ten-year, roughly 4-billion-mile (6.4 billion km) journey, the Rosetta space probe finally got to within 62 miles (100 km) of its target, Comet 67P/C-G. Rosetta dropped a small probe, called Philae, onto the comet, which then bounced several times before landing. It sent back a large amount of data to scientists on Earth.

From right to left —the Roman god Jupiter, his wife Juno, and the astronomer Galileo.

3

= THE NUMBER OF ALUMINUM LEGO FIGURES CARRIED ONBOARD THE JUNO SPACE PROBE. IT WAS PART OF THE BRICKS IN SPACE PROJECT, DESIGNED TO INCREASE CHILDREN'S AWARENESS OF SPACE EXPLORATION.

LANDERS AND ROVERS

The first space probes to reach a planet or moon were deliberately crash-landed by scientists on the surface because they didn't have the technology to make a cushioned landing. Modern probes have been accidentally damaged during descending or landing—the riskiest moments in a space probe's journey. But some have survived to send back vital information.

Smash!

The spectacular Deep Impact mission sent a space probe blasting into the nucleus, or solid part, of a comet called Tempel 1. The probe smashed into the comet at a speed of 23,000 miles per hour (37,000 kmh) sending up a cloud of material from the comet's nucleus, and creating a 492-foot- (150 m) wide crater.

This image was taken 67 seconds after Deep Impact's space probe crashed into Tempel 1.

HOW DO PROBES LAND?

Once close to its target, gravity pulls a lander probe toward a planet's or moon's surface. It will speed up unless some form of braking device is employed. Parachutes, jet thrusters, or a skycrane all help the probe to land softly.

PIGGYBACK PROBES

Some lander probes, such as the Philae probe, hitch a ride on a bigger orbiter probe before being dropped to the surface. Huygens was a probe released from the Cassini orbiter in 2005. It landed on Saturn's moon, Titan—over 745.6 million miles (1.2 billion km) from Earth.

Roving Around

A rover is a space probe that can move around the surface of a planet or a moon. The first successful rover was the car-sized Lunakhod 1. It landed on the Moon in 1970 and was controlled remotely by scientists from the Soviet Union.

These models show three series of Mars rovers. The real rovers are still on Mars!

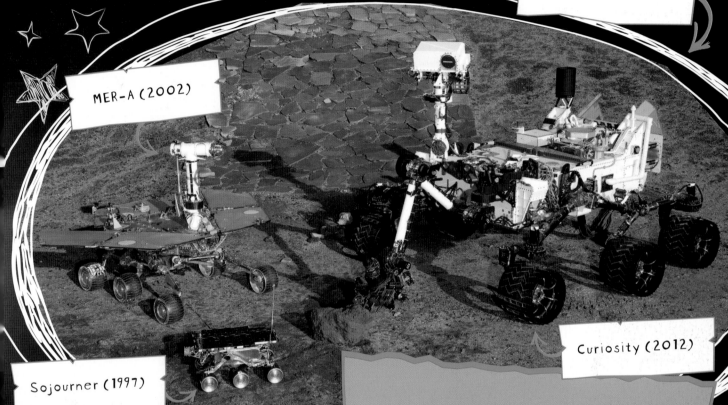

MER-A (2002)

Sojourner (1997)

Curiosity (2012)

MARS MOVERS

Viking 1 and 2 were the first lander probes on Mars. They have been followed by three generations of Mars rovers. Sojourner was the first. It landed in 1997 and was about 26 inches (65 cm) long. It was followed in 2002 by the MER-A and MER-B rovers (5.4 feet (1.65 m) long), and Curiosity in 2012 (9.8 feet (3 m) long).

36,700

= THE NUMBER OF PHOTOS THAT CURIOSITY TOOK DURING ITS FIRST YEAR ON MARS. TO CELEBRATE ONE YEAR ON THE PLANET, IT EVEN PLAYED "HAPPY BIRTHDAY" TO ITSELF— THE FIRST KNOWN MUSIC ON MARS!

SPACE MEN AND WOMEN

With a cry of, "Poyekhali!" ("Off we go!"), Russian Yuri Gagarin blasted off in his 7.5-foot- (2.3 m) wide Vostok 1 spacecraft in 1961 to become the first person in space. More than 500 astronauts from around the world have followed Gagarin, including 26-year-old Valentina Tereshkova, the first woman in space, in 1963.

Men On The Moon

Twelve astronauts have set foot on the Moon as part of NASA's Apollo missions (1969-72). These were extraordinarily complex missions, powered by an onboard computer with just 64 kilobytes of memory—half a million times less memory than today's smartphone!

Neil Armstrong took this photo of his fellow astronaut Buzz Aldrin during the Apollo 11 moon landing in 1969.

20—30

= THE NUMBER OF SECONDS' WORTH OF FUEL LEFT IN APOLLO II'S LANDING MODULE AS IT LANDED ON THE MOON'S SURFACE. NEIL ARMSTRONG AND EDWIN "BUZZ" ALDRIN BECAME THE FIRST ASTRONAUTS TO SET FOOT ON THE MOON.

SPACE TOURISTS

A handful of people who were not fully trained astronauts have paid large amounts of money to travel into space. The first, Dennis Tito, spent almost eight days on board the International **Space Station** in 2001. A number of companies are developing their own private spacecraft to give people a taste of space in the future.

Suited and Booted

A spacesuit is a mini survival capsule that protects an astronaut from the extremes of heat, cold, and harmful radiation in space. NASA's Extravehicular Mobility Unit (EMU) suit is made up of 13 layers and weighs 280 lbs (127 kg) on Earth. It can take up to an hour to put on and features liquid-cooled underwear, a backpack that recycles air for the astronaut to breathe, and gloves with heated fingertips.

SPACEWALKS

Extra-vehicular Activity (EVA), or spacewalks, are when astronauts leave the safety of their spacecraft and go out into space. Nearly all spacewalkers remain attached to the spacecraft by a line or other connector, which supplies oxygen and electrical power to their EVA spacesuit.

Bruce McCandless enjoys a wild EVA using a Manned Maneuvering Unit (MMU). This jetpack fires nitrogen gas through 24 jet nozzles so the astronaut can change direction in space.

NASA Diaper

Spacewalking astronauts wear a Maximum Absorbency Garment while in space. This is a high-tech adult diaper that can absorb up to 2.1 quarts (2 L) of fluid.

WHEN WAS THE FIRST EVA?

The first EVA was performed by Russian cosmonaut Alexei Leonov in 1965. It lasted 12 minutes.

ASTRONAUT TRAINING

There's a huge amount of training that has to be done before an astronaut can strap in for lift-off. Astronauts need to be physically fit and mentally sharp.

Know Your Way Around

Every astronaut has to be familiar with the controls and procedures of their spacecraft. This training can last months or even years. Training takes place in realistic models of the spacecraft. Every part of the job, from how to put on a spacesuit to what to do in an emergency situation, must be learned and practiced.

DEALING WITH MICROGRAVITY

In space, astronauts have to deal with **microgravity**, also called zero gravity. In microgravity, people experience weightlessness and will float. This can make the body lose its sense of direction, so trainee astronauts get to experience weightlessness beforehand in aircraft nicknamed "vomit comets." They are regular planes that fly up and down sharply to create 20–30-second periods of weightlessness.

These astronauts are training in a "vomit comet."

Going Swimmingly

Astronauts at NASA (National Aeronautics and Space Administration) get to train in the world's largest indoor swimming pool. The Neutral Buoyancy Lab is 202 feet (61.6 m) by 102 feet (31.1m) and is 40 feet (12.2m) deep. The tank holds full-size models of spacecraft and allows astronauts to practice some of the movements needed to perform a spacewalk.

803

= THE NUMBER OF DAYS SPENT IN SPACE BY RUSSIA'S SERGEI KRIKALEV, WHO HAS LIVED ONBOARD FOUR DIFFERENT CRAFT: SOYUZ, SPACE SHUTTLE, AND THE MIR AND ISS SPACE STATIONS.

MISSION SPECIALISTS

Most astronauts are either talented scientists or jet pilots. Each has their own special tasks to perform during the mission, such as running experiments inside the spacecraft or operating a giant robot arm to move equipment in space. Many astronauts are cross-trained so they can also perform other crew members' tasks.

Astronauts train underwater at the Neutral Buoyancy Lab.

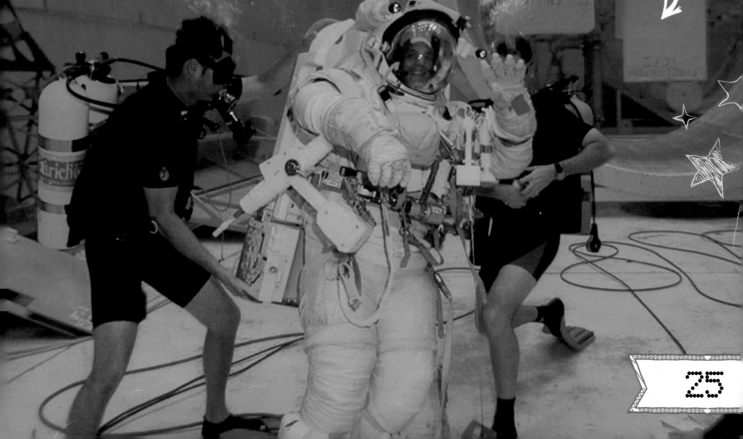

THE INTERNATIONAL SPACE STATION

Look up! Over 249 miles (400 km) above Earth, the biggest ever piece of space hardware orbits our planet once every 90 minutes. The International Space Station (ISS) was built by a partnership of 16 countries. It is 242 feet (74 m) long and 360 feet (110 m) wide, a little bigger than a football field.

Piece-By-Piece

The ISS was flown into space, piece by piece, starting in 1998. Gradually, new modules and parts have been added to its central spine, including eight pairs of giant solar-array wings (SAWs). Each SAW contains 32,800 solar cells that convert energy from the Sun into electricity to power the ISS.

ONE BIG BUILDING SITE

The ISS was space's biggest building site, requiring giant robot arms, many space flights, and over 1,100 hours of spacewalks by 113 different astronauts to complete. The longest single EVA was by Susan J. Helms and James S. Voss in 2001, which lasted 8 hours and 56 minutes.

This is a view of the ISS from the Space Shuttle Atlantis.

Roomy

ISS crews work and relax in modules, or sections, which provide as much living space as a six-bedroom house. The ISS includes a gym, two bathrooms, and docking points for the spacecraft that ferry crew, supplies, and parts to and from the ISS. The crew can admire the view from the cupola, a 360° window, and even surf the Web and post on social media from space!

ISS crews are made up of six or seven people. This crew is enjoying a zero-gravity meal!

The ISS weighs 926,000 pounds (420,000 kg), equal to more than 300 cars on Earth.

While on an EVA outside of the ISS in 2008, astronaut Heide Stefanyshyn-Piper lost her grip on her high-tech tool bag, which floated away. The bag, which contained about $100,000 of equipment, burned up in Earth's atmosphere a year later.

SERIOUS SCIENCE

It's not all fun onboard the ISS. As a semi-permanent base in space, the space station allows astronauts to investigate both Earth and space and perform hundreds of science experiments on the long-term effects on people, plants, and materials of being in space.

144
= THE NUMBER OF SPACECRAFT FLIGHTS TO THE INTERNATIONAL SPACE STATION BETWEEN 1998 AND 2014.

LIFE IN SPACE

Some of the science experiments onboard manned spacecraft have focused on the astronauts themselves. They have taught us about space's effects on the human body and helped us understand how to equip astronauts for long missions away from Earth.

Space Side Effects

Astronauts can lose their sense of direction and feel sick in their first few days in space. The lack of gravity makes blood rise in their bodies from the legs into the chest and head. This gives astronauts a puffy face and sometimes leads to sinus pain and congestion.

KEEPING FIT

Without the gravity found on Earth, an astronaut's muscles grow weaker because they are not required to support the body. The ISS is equipped with a weight machine, as well as a treadmill and exercise bike, to help astronauts maintain muscle strength on a long mission. The crew exercises for 2–3 hours each day.

Russian cosmonaut Maxim Suraev exercises on the treadmill on the ISS.

2 (5)
= THE TYPICAL AMOUNT IN INCHES (CM) THAT AN ASTRONAUT GROWS TALLER IN SPACE, DUE TO THE LACK OF GRAVITY PUSHING DOWN ON THEIR SPINE.

Food For Thought

Early astronaut food was crushed into a soft paste and eaten squeezed from toothpaste-like tubes. Today, many foods are dried to save weight and sealed in pouches. The food has to be rehydrated, or have water added back in, and heated. Food is eaten off a dinner tray that has straps so it can be attached to a wall or table to stop it from floating away.

This is what a meal on the ISS looks like. The utensils are magnetic to keep them from floating off the tray.

HOW DO YOU "GO" IN SPACE?

Very carefully! Space toilets use flowing air rather than water to flush away the waste liquid and solids. On the ISS, the liquid waste is filtered and cleaned and then used again as drinking water. The solid waste is kept in bags in a storage container until the spacecraft returns to Earth.

CLEANING UP

In the microgravity of space, water doesn't run downward like it does on Earth. It floats in all directions and can damage onboard computers. To help astronauts keep clean, scientists have developed toothpaste and shampoo that do not need to be rinsed out. Instead of running water, astronauts use damp cloths to clean themselves on the ISS.

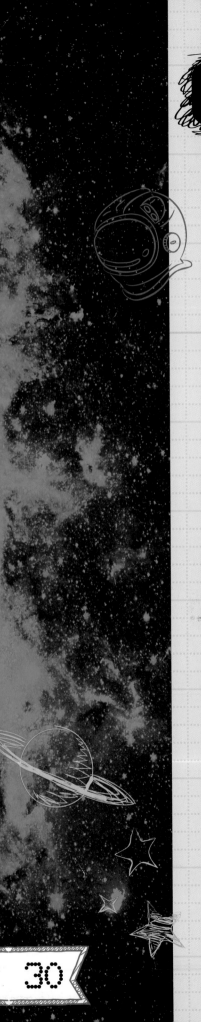

GLOSSARY

aperture The opening at the front of a telescope, camera, or other instrument that lets in light or other waves

atmosphere The gases surrounding the surface of a planet

black hole An object in space with such strong gravity that nothing nearby can escape its pull, including light

concave Having a curved, inward shape, like a bowl

exoplanet A planet found outside of the solar system

gravity The invisible force of attraction between objects

light-year The distance traveled by light in one year (approximately 6 trillion miles (9.65 trillion km))

matter Substances that exist as solids, liquids, or gases

microgravity The very weak pull of gravity that makes astronauts and objects in space feel weightless.

orbit To travel around another object in space, often in an elliptical path

payload The cargo carried by a rocket or another launch vehicle from Earth into space

radiation Energy that travels through space in waves, such as infrared, X-rays, and visible light

reflecting A telescope that uses mirrors to reflect and focus light

refracting A telescope that uses lenses to focus light

space probe A machine sent into space to explore and send back information

space station A spacecraft designed to house humans in space, often for long periods of time. The International Space Station is one example in use now.

thrust The power used to push something forward

FURTHER INFORMATION

Books

Go Figure: A Math Journey Through Space
by Anne Rooney (Crabtree, 2014)

How to be a Space Explorer:
Your Out-of-this-World Adventure
by Lonely Planet (Lonely Planet Kids Publishing, 2014)

Exploring Space Travel
by Laura Hamilton (Waxman Lerner, 2011.)

Websites

http://amazing-space.stsci.edu/resources/
 explorations/groundup/

A visual history of telescopes and how they
have developed

http://coolcosmos.ipac.caltech.edu/

A guide and gallery of infrared objects in space

www.nasa.gov/mission_pages/station/main/
 #.VDZmZfldXHk

NASA's detailed Web pages on the International
Space Station

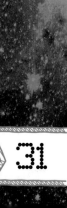

INDEX